Let's Go Have Fun!

by Jana Martin

PEARSON

Scott
Foresman

Editorial Offices: Glenview, Illinois • Parsippany, New Jersey • New York, New York
Sales Offices: Needham, Massachusetts • Duluth, Georgia • Glenview, Illinois
Coppell, Texas • Ontario, California • Mesa, Arizona

ISBN: 0-328-13396-5

8 9 10 V0G1 14 13 12 11 10 09 08

F-U-N!

F-U-N! This book is all about having fun. What kind of fun? Well, maybe not the kind of fun you have every day. Mrs. Garcia teaches third grade, and she loves to show people how to have fun.

Now, Mrs. Garcia's fun is not the kind of fun you have at home. It's not playing a video game or watching television.

So what kind of fun is she talking about? Turn the pages and you'll see!

Photos from Mrs. Garcia's scrapbook

When Mrs. Garcia was your age, she lived on a farm. Almost everyone was a farmer where she grew up. Her family raised hogs and cattle. Every summer, all the kids got really excited because the state fair was coming to town!

The state fair meant three things. First, there was a giant amusement park with many thrilling rides. Second, there were contests galore, in which judges decided who had grown the biggest pumpkin, who had raised the prettiest calf, or who could eat the most pie.

Third, there was row after row of food stalls, where vendors sold everything from grilled corn on the cob to corn dogs to popcorn.

Amusement park rides add to the excitement of state fairs.

Today most states hold a state fair, often in the state's capital city. You can spend the whole day and night there and never get bored. For many, the rides are the best part.

When the state fair comes to town, the organizers set up Ferris wheels, roller coasters, and even a log flume ride. State fairs are a great form of **recreation** for the entire family. It's amazing how a state fair can take an empty field and turn it into a full-scale amusement park!

Squashing the Competition

Mrs. Garcia likes to talk about the year she and her brother came home from the state fair with two blue ribbons. She won for having the best-looking hog. Her brother won for eating the most pie! It wasn't much fun for him later, though . . . he felt pretty sick!

Many states have been holding fairs for more than 150 years. Each state fair has its own unique, quirky events. Mississippi, for example, boasts a Biscuit Booth, with 50,000 biscuits. Recently, Massachusetts proudly displayed a 920-pound pumpkin in its Vegetable Building. The homespun quality is part of the magic of state fairs.

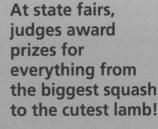

At state fairs, judges award prizes for everything from the biggest squash to the cutest lamb!

State Fair Trivia

State fairs have been the birthplace of some wacky creations. Take a look at some state-fair firsts.

Called Spun Sugar, cotton candy first appeared at state fairs.

Corn dogs were first sold at state fairs. Today, there are dozens of food-on-a-stick items featured at state fairs, including alligator and deep-fried candy.

In 1807, Elkanah Watson introduced the first state fair. He showed off his sheep in the public square in Pittsfield, Massachusetts.

In 1903, the dairy industry began creating butter sculptures for state fairs. They molded barnyard scenes and celebrities out of solid butter. One cow sculpture used over 800 pounds of butter. Today, butter sculptures are often molded around a wire or wooden frame.

In the 1940s, an amazing new kind of oven, called the Radarange, was introduced at a state fair. It could bake a potato in six minutes. Today, these amazing ovens can be found in many homes. They're known as microwave ovens!

Nature's Show!

State fairs were designed to show off each state's biggest and best farm crops and cleverest inventions, but sometimes it's nature that puts on the best show of all. National and state parks can often provide huge amounts of fun.

The most **spectacular** thing Mrs. Garcia ever saw was in Yellowstone National Park, in Montana. Among the many natural

U.S. National and State Parks

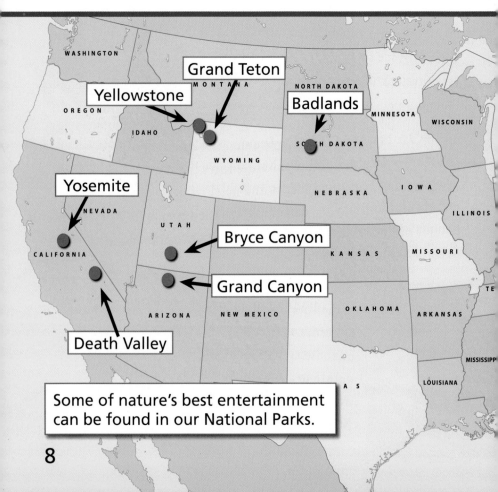

Some of nature's best entertainment can be found in our National Parks.

wonders in the park are the more than 500 **geysers**—underground springs that shoot out blasts of hot water and steam. The most famous geyser in the park—and maybe in the world—is Old Faithful.

People gather outside and wait for Old Faithful to erupt. The geyser has been shooting out blasts for a long, long time. Each eruption shoots thousands of gallons of boiling water, hundreds of feet high! It's quite an exciting sight to see.

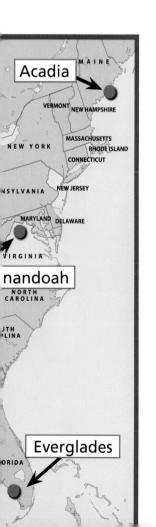

Old Faithful erupts
about every 76 minutes.

Leagues of Fun

What's better than cheering on your favorite team? How about playing with your favorite team! There's nothing like being part of a team when it comes to fun. Little League baseball is one of the all-time classic American sports. When Mrs. Garcia was growing up, Little League was just for boys. Now girls can play, too, and they're slugging and sliding with the best of them!

Little League is actually a national organization, but for the regular season, players compete within their own towns. The whole town gets involved, with local businesses sponsoring teams.

Little League games and other sporting events bring families out to cheer for their team.

League Champions!

Of course, you've all heard that baseball is just a game, and winning isn't everything. But for many winning certainly is something! The thrill of hearing family and friends cheering as you round the bases is immensely exciting.

In Little League, the winning team in each town competes in a regional **championship**. Eventually, the top teams in the United States compete at the World Series in Pennsylvania. There they play teams from all over the world. The games are shown on national television and viewed by millions of fans.

Teams from Latin America, Asia, and even Africa compete in Little League championships. Little League has come a long way since its beginnings in 1938.

Today, boys and girls around the world enjoy playing sports. Competing in team sports teaches youngsters the importance of being physically active and playing by the rules. In the end, though, the best part of team sports is the friendships you build with your teammates. It's fun to get cheers from your family and neighbors too.

Sometimes skateboarding seems to go against gravity. But gravity is the secret force behind all skateboarding tricks.

Not Your Parents' Skateboarding!

Skateboarding is no longer what it once was. Long ago, skateboards were homemade, with roller-skate wheels attached to a plank of wood.

Now skateboarding is an entirely different ballgame! Skateboarders perform moves called *ollies, McTwists,* and *caballerials*. Watch as the skater flips, spins and turns, and you'll see gravity at work. Gravity holds the skateboard in place with the force of nature.

One of the sport's most famous skateboarders is Tony Hawk. Tony became a professional skateboarder at the age of 14. Throughout his career he has competed in more than one hundred competitions—most of which he has won!

Today skateboarding is popular in cities and suburbs around the world. Communities have built skateboarding parks, with ramps and half-pipes. Clearly, helmets are not optional!

Mrs. Garcia brought her friend Jake to answer your questions and teach you some skateboarding moves. Of course, you'll need practice, safety equipment, and supervision to try these moves.

"So, Jake, how do you do it?"

"Practice, practice, practice," laughs Jake. "I started out just trying to balance on my skateboard. Next, I worked on moving on a straight, smooth surface.

"The easiest trick to start with is probably the ollie, named after Alan 'Ollie' Gelfand who invented the move in 1970. You tap the tail of the board on the ground in order to jump. Once you can do the ollie, you can do many other moves."

Extreme sports like skateboarding have been catching on across the country.

15

Please DO Touch These Exhibits

Museums have many great **exhibits**, but it can be frustrating when they are set off by velvet ropes. There are so many "Do Not Touch" signs and guards hushing you! Well, not all museums are like that. **Interactive** museums encourage people to touch, or even walk through, their exhibits! An interactive museum is definitely more fun.

Let's take a visit to Chicago's Museum of Science and Industry, the largest science museum in the United States. Yearly, over four million visitors troop through its halls. Let's go through some of the exhibits.

A popular exhibit at the Museum of Science and Industry is "The Heart." You can listen to the *lub-dub* sound the heart makes as you walk through the model. At 16 feet tall, it shows what a real human heart looks like—inside and out! As you walk through, you become a drop of blood working your way through the human heart.

Now let's get a firsthand look at what life was like a hundred years ago. "Yesterday's Main Street" is an exhibit where you can stroll along the cobblestone streets of 1910!

Which came first, the chicken or the egg? This exhibit might not solve that riddle, but it does give an up-close look at what happens inside an egg. Those baby chicks are so cute when they peck their way out!

Going to a movie is fun, but seeing how a movie is made is even more fun with "Action! An Adventure in Movie Making." You can learn how films are chosen for production and how a studio set becomes a city street. You can see how amazing stunts are performed and how makeup turns actors into aliens. You also get to make your own film that you can take home.

Of course, where would the movies be without screenwriters? Screenwriters tell stories either based on novels or plays or using their own original ideas. In the "Meet the Moviemakers" exhibit, you'll get to see authentic movie scripts from some of your favorite movies.

A thermal image of a man is projected onto a wall at the Museum of Science and Industry

Under the Big Top

When Mrs. Garcia was young, she would daydream about running away and joining the circus. Doesn't that sound like great fun? You don't need to run away with a circus to learn tricks from professionals, however.

Circus Juventas is one of several major circus schools for kids in the United States. This circus school is in St. Paul, Minnesota. Students from three years old and up take classes in **acrobatics**, clowning, juggling, and tightrope walking. Some of these children have gone on to join professional circuses. Most just enjoy developing their skills and performing locally.

Emily Platt and her brother Charlie have been performing with Circus Juventus for several years. Take a look under the Big Top to see some of the skills they learn at circus school.

Time for
Circus School

Now Try This

You have learned about some of the great forms of recreation and entertainment available. You know that they can be found at baseball parks and national parks, at museums and circus schools.

Now, it's your turn to find out more about places to have fun! You may know of some in your state or community. There may be others you've always wanted to explore. This is your chance!

The Apostle Islands National Park is known for its kayaking.

Use the Internet to find out about different places you can go to be entertained. Jot down a few notes about each place. Then, when you are finished, create a travel poster to share what you have discovered.

The chart below lists places under four categories of entertainment. These are some suggestions to get you started. Feel free to explore the places you come up with on your own. Don't forget—have fun!

It's All Fun!

Museums	Performing Arts	Sports Destinations	The Great Outdoors
Age of Steam Railroad Museum, Dallas, Texas	Mann's Chinese Theater, Hollywood Walk of Fame, Los Angeles, California	Kane County Cougars, Geneva, Illinois	Mammoth Cave, Park City, Kentucky
Asian Art Museum, Seattle, Washington	Joffrey Ballet, New York, New York	Long Beach Aquatic Festival, Long Beach, California	Broadmoor Wildlife Sanctuary, Natich, Maine
Negro Leagues Baseball Museum, Kansas City, Missouri	Children's Chorus of Maryland, Towson, Maryland	Appalachian Beach Volleyball, Luck, North Carolina	Apostle Island National Park, Bayfield, Wisconsin

Glossary

acrobatics *n.* the skills or performance routines of an acrobat.

championship *n.* the final stage of a sports tournament or competition.

exhibits *n.* displays of objects of interest, especially in museums.

geysers *n.* underground springs that spew steam from the Earth.

interactive *adj.* allowing the exchange of information between a person and a machine.

recreation *n.* an activity that a person does for fun.

spectacular *adj.* impressive or dramatic to watch.